CREATING A LIFE OF JOY
A MEDITATIVE GUIDE

SALLE MERRILL REDFIELD
Author of *The Joy of Meditating*

I would like to gratefully acknowledge the following author and publisher who have granted permission to use excerpts from the following work:

From *THE CELESTINE PROPHECY* by James Redfield.
Copyright © 1993 by James Redfield. By permission of Warner Books.

This is an adaptation of *CREATING A LIFE OF JOY.*
Copyright © 1999 by Salle Merrill Redfield
All Rights Reserved.
Adaptation approved by the Author.

Abridgement approved by the Author.
Copyright Ⓟ by Time Warner AudioBooks
Copyright © Time Warner AudioBooks (packaging elements only)
A division of Time Warner Trade Publishing,
1271 Avenue of the Americas, New York, NY 10020
Manufactured in the U.S.A.
Selection #2-32768

First Printing: December 1999
10 9 8 7 6 5 4 3 2 1

Cover and Book Design by Platinum Design, Inc.
Produced by Maja Thomas and Salle Merrill Redfield
Directed by Maja Thomas
Text Adapted for Audio by Judith McGuinn
Production Coordinated by Daniel Metcalf
Original Music by Peter Kater of Earthsea Music
Photographs: Images Ⓡ Copyright 1999 PhotoDisc, Inc.
"Boom Box" Photo (pg. 4) by Karen Cera
"The Alhambra" Photo (pg. 13) © Corel

SALLE MERRILL REDFIELD is the author of the bestseller *THE JOY OF MEDITATING.* She also wrote and recorded the audio programs *THE JOY OF MEDITATING, THE CELESTINE MEDITATIONS,* and *MEDITATIONS FOR THE TENTH INSIGHT.* Salle lectures internationally on creating a joyful, purpose-filled life. A native of Alabama, she resides in Florida with her husband, James Redfield.

Salle writes a monthly column online in *THE CELESTINE JOURNAL.* It is accessible on her Web site: www.celestinevision.com.

Joy is the holy fire that keeps our
purpose warm and our intelligence aglow.
—Helen Keller

There comes a point in each of our lives
when we realize that we are
responsible for our own joy.

HAVING THE DAY-TO-DAY
JOY WE LONG FOR
COMES FROM
UNDERSTANDING OUR
BASIC HUMAN NEEDS

—FROM FINDING FOOD
AND SHELTER TO
FINDING PURPOSE AND
SELF-ACTUALIZATION

—AND THEN DEVELOPING
WAYS TO MEET THEM.

The challenge comes when we try to find our unique style
for meeting our needs in positive ways.

become an expert

in how you are

meeting your needs.

If there is something you

really love to do, ask yourself

which of your basic needs

are being met.

Do you limit yourself because of certain
unconscious or outdated beliefs?
Take time to explore your beliefs and
how they originated.

Learn to play. Relax. Try new things. Connect with the beauty of the world.
Take time to appreciate your many assets. Make each day special.
Prepare for more joyful beliefs and experiences in your life.

When we set

goals and

work toward

accomplishing

them, our

interest in life

is heightened

as we anticipate

a brighter

tomorrow.

WHEN WE HAVE A CLEAR VISION OF WHAT WE WANT
AND COMMIT TO HAVING IT,
OUR DREAMS CAN COME TRUE.

EACH TIME WE COMPLETE A GOAL,
WE DEVELOP MORE SELF-ESTEEM
AND A GREATER SENSE OF THE
CREATIVE PROCESS.

Ask yourself,
"If I were living a
life that brought
me the most joy
and purpose, what
would it be like?"

Honor your responses.
You may see an image of the future.
Analyze the information that comes
to you and find a way to incorporate
it into your life.

Resist becoming too invested
in achieving your goals in some preconceived way.
Many paths can lead to the
same destination.

Every step counts
along the way to our goals.
Celebrate even the
smallest accomplishments.
You are actively doing
what it takes to create
your life the way you
want it to be.

WE ALL
GO THROUGH
CYCLES
WHERE
THERE IS
MORE TO
GET DONE
THAN WE
CAN HANDLE.
WE BEGIN
TO TAKE
CARE OF
WHAT'S
MOST URGENT
INSTEAD
OF WHAT'S
MOST
IMPORTANT.

Create a strategy for prioritizing your time

and organizing your personal space. Consider your goals.
Make sure you have enough time to pursue them—as well as
to handle your existing responsibilities.

To create a joyful life, you need to communicate effectively.
You will be challenged to bridge barriers of thought, to reach across
differing backgrounds, and to reconcile conflicting definitions so that
you can understand and be understood.

Too often in conversation, we
focus, not on what the other
person is saying, but on
what we are going to say in
response. The first step in
communication is listening.

You need to listen

"deeply" for the clues that

show us the meaning beneath

the words. When you listen deeply

to others, they feel validated

and understood.

You must remember that
we each have our own beliefs
and assumptions about the nature of life
formed through years of experience.

BE CAREFUL NOT TO LET
COMMUNICATION BECOME
MANIPULATIVE:"OUR PARTICULAR
STYLE OF CONTROLLING
OTHERS IS ONE WE LEARNED IN
CHILDHOOD TO GET ATTENTION,
TO GET THE ENERGY MOVING
OUR WAY, AND WE'RE STUCK THERE.
THIS STYLE IS SOMETHING WE
REPEAT OVER AND OVER AGAIN.
I CALL IT OUR UNCONSCIOUS
CONTROL DRAMA."

—JAMES REDFIELD *The Celestine Prophecy*

Take a higher stance.
Stay centered.
You don't have to win.
You can be the one who
takes responsibility
and brings the relationship
back to authenticity.

When you lead
from a place
of inner strength
and peace
you become a truly
effective communicator.

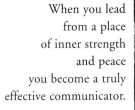

Of all the elements of creating a life of joy,
achieving a state of inner peace is most important.

You can begin to feel inner peace when you have a sense of mental control and clarity.

YOU CAN ENHANCE YOUR
SENSE OF JOY BY FINDING AN
EXPERIENCE THAT HELPS TO
QUIET YOUR MIND WHILE IT
HELPS YOU TO SEE THAT WE
ARE ALL PART OF A GREATER
DESIGN. SOME PEOPLE FIND IT
THROUGH MEDITATION.

What we say to ourselves has a profound effect on our sense of peace,
even more so than what others say to us.

When you speak to yourself
in encouraging ways,
you become more forgiving
and gentle with others.

Stop worrying about
what you can't control.
Take action when it's possible.
Find a way to release the rest.

*Let yourself
off the hook.*

*We are all souls in growth.
There is something miraculous
about the process of forgiveness.*

The most important source
    of inner peace
        is our connection with the sacred.

Connection begins with
the act of intention.
You have to knock
on the door.

Great mystics tell us:
God is in all things.
Everything we once took for granted
has more presence when
we seek its divinity.

Once
it occurs, our
connection with
God feels like
coming home.

WE NO LONGER FEEL
ISOLATED IN
A UNIVERSE THAT IS
MEANINGLESS
AND UNCARING.
INSTEAD WE FEEL THE
DEEP PEACE OF
KNOWING WE ARE
LOVED AND GUIDED.

Life is full of coincidences.
Psychologist Carl Jung defined
meaningful coincidences as
"synchronicity."

THE MIRACLE OF SYNCHRONICITY CAN BEGIN WITH INTUITION. A TRUE INTUITION CAN GUIDE YOU—IT IS ABOUT GROWING AND EXPANDING.

If you follow
your intuition,
you may experience
an event that
makes your life
better or somehow
leads you in a
different direction.

open up

to the sacred.

Begin to act on
the opportunities
that are presented.

We are each born with
        a spiritual mission.
Once we awaken to it,
        our lives take on
a higher meaning.
        We begin to fulfill
our inner potential.

THE DARKEST FEAR OF LIFE

OFTEN COMES JUST BEFORE

THE JOY OF DISCOVERING

OUR SPIRITUAL MISSION.

WE ARE MERELY AWAKENING

AND RESTRUCTURING OUR

LIVES TO BE MORE WHOLE.

You can listen to the deep knowing you have inside that tells you what you are here to do.

Gaining clarity about your mission also comes from a thoughtful exploration of your past. No one has ever before been on earth who has exactly your experience or your distinct view of the world.

See your life as a whole.
What does it prepare you
to teach others about leading
a fuller more spiritual life?

This is the
true joy in life…
being used for a purpose
recognized by yourself as
a mighty one…I am of the
opinion that my life belongs
to the whole community
and, as long as I live, it is
my privilege to do for it
whatever I can. Life is no
brief candle to me. It's sort
of a splendid torch which
I've got to hold up for the
moment, and I want to
make it burn as brightly as
possible before handing
it on to future generations.

—GEORGE BERNARD SHAW

Joyful living must be an attitude
that is thoroughly integrated
into your day-to-day activities.

You must want to have more joy in your life and consistently hold a vision of the experience.

Your
life is important.
If you take the time to
help one individual, to
communicate honestly
and authentically, the
effect cannot be
measured.

and makes this world a better, more spiritual place. Real Joy is secured when we put all the pieces together into one conscious life journey that touches others

Make joy a priority…

and you will find levels of experience and satisfaction that you have never even imagined.

Information about the CD

The CD included in this
volume contains seven
meditations based on
principles from
Salle Merrill Redfield's book
CREATING A LIFE OF JOY.
Each meditation is led by the
author. The CD is bookmarked
at the commencement of each
ten-minute meditation and
every five minutes throughout.

These meditations are
included as text in the trade
paperback version of
CREATING A LIFE OF JOY
(0-446-67587-3) and are also
available as audio in the
abridged audiobook version of
CREATING A LIFE OF JOY.
(1-57042-768-2).